Stories From a North Dakota Cheerleader

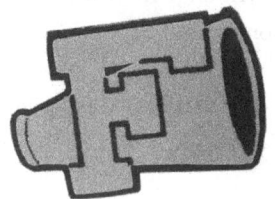

Carol Owen Reynolds

Stories From a North Dakota Cheerleader
Carol Owen Reynolds
Published August 2023
Heirloom Editions
Imprint of Jan-Carol Publishing, Inc.
All rights reserved
Copyright © 2023 Carol Owen Reynolds
Cover photograph of cheerleader circa 1958 by Ed Weiss, photographer, during the time of the *Wells County Free Press*.

This book may not be reproduced in whole or part, in any manner whatsoever without written permission, with the exception of brief quotations within book reviews or articles.

ISBN: 978-1-954978-98-0
Library of Congress Control Number: 2023945013

You may contact the publisher:
Jan-Carol Publishing, Inc.
PO Box 701
Johnson City, TN 37605
publisher@jancarolpublishing.com
www.jancarolpublishing.com

To my dear life-long friend, Lucy Schimke Bell. She has stood by me since my mom introduced me to her just after she was born. We started school and church together. We graduated high school together. Her dad offered to pay for my college expenses if I would just stay in North Dakota and continue to go to school with her. When I needed someone to talk to, she was there. When praise for one of us was handed out, we were together. When I wanted to go somewhere, my parents would ask, "Is Lucille going?" It got to the point where I asked, "Does she always have to be with me?"

When I began writing this book, she helped doing the editing and believe me, she was a tough editor. How can you thank a friend of 80 plus years? I love and respect her for all she has done for me, even outside being a critic for this book!

Table of Contents

A Stormy Birth..1
May Day..4
The Night Before Christmas in Fessenden..8
It's Fair Time!..11
Summers and the Jim River..17
The Fight..20
Glenn..24
Surprise!...28
Loss of a Child..32
My Uncle Arnie..39
I'm in Jail!..42
Ms. Macbeth..47
Surgery Awry!..51
A Big Heart..54
Terms & Definitions 58
Acknowledgments 61

A Stormy Birth

*"If you don't expect anything,
you'll never be disappointed!"*
— Famous Emma sayings

Everything is planned and in place. Their second baby is on the way. Emma and Newt know exactly how it will happen. Their first child, Nate, is already staying with his Aunt Ida and Uncle Bill. The real bonus is that his cousins, Marlys and Beverly, get to help take care of him. They love chasing two-year-old Nate around the house on the cold January days and messing up his beautiful blonde curly hair. Everyone in Fessenden says what a cute kid he is and love those blonde curls.

The farm, although six miles out of town, has good roads and the additional seventeen miles out of Fessenden to the Harvey Hospital should not take more than half an hour once the labor pains started, but the storm had gotten a jump start a couple hours sooner and the snow piled up quickly.

Newt decided to get the car warmed up even though the pains are only about half an hour apart. He ran back in the house after trying to start the car for several minutes and announced, "The damn car won't start!" Emma suggests he try starting the truck but it, too, is frozen solid in the outdoor shed and she says, "There's only one thing we can do: try to get to the tracks and flag down the train." The tracks are across the yard, over the road and through the ditch.

They bundle up and start off on their journey to try and catch the train, due in a few minutes. Newt says, "Good thing you got those high top overshoes." She crept carefully over the edge of the road and began sinking in the snow-filled ditch. Then, another step, and she sank in even further. The third step sank her in up to the top of her legs and she had to reach out for assistance to take the next step and sank in again and again.

Newt tries to help her and still maintain control of the lantern that they needed desperately to flag down the train. They saw the faint light of the train in the distance and he started swinging the lantern. As the train got closer, it blared the whistle, acknowledging they were seen.

Emma struggled to raise her leg and start up the steps of the caboose. It seemed her leg had frozen like an icicle and wouldn't bend. Newt cradled her rear while still maintaining control of the lantern and shoved her up the steps. As the train started back up the tracks, Emma felt the pains coming faster. "Do you have enough money to get the cigars for the other men?" He said, "What a stupid thing to say right now! Yes, I have enough money and I can't get them anyway until you have the baby so I know if it should say it's a boy or it's a girl because that's the way they print the cigars. The most important thing you need to be worried about is keeping that kid inside you until we get to the hospital."

By the time the train arrived in Harvey, the pains were coming faster. She tried to keep her body from bearing down each time a pain hit her but it was no use. Newt asked the train conductor, "How far is the hospital?" The conductor said, "It's about half a mile but she can't make it. The streets here in Harvey are too icy and I doubt she wants to deliver that baby after falling in the street!" Newt hollered back, "There she goes! She's hard headed and determined to get there!"

Luckily, Dr. Boyum was at the hospital and he began his instructions to the nurse, "Get a stretcher! We got a baby coming! Help her up! Don't worry about her coat and boots! Just cut off her underpants!

We are running out of time! I can see the baby's head!" Newt, stunned, turned his head away from Emma and said, "It must be another boy. I don't see any blonde curls."

Dr. Boyum goes to work delivering the baby and says, "Too bad, Newt, it's a girl and she's bald as a pool cue!" Newt said, "I don't care if she doesn't have any hair. She can wear a bonnet while I spoil her rotten." They signed the birth certificate two days later and looked forward to picking Nate up at Bill and Ida's house in Fessenden.

(Published December 31, 2022 in *The Herald-Press*, Harvey, ND.)

Cousins Marlys Owen and Carol Owen

May Day
(Fessenden, North Dakota Style)

"He thinks she's a cat's pajamas."
— Famous Emma Sayings

May First, May Day, was always a day of great celebration in our little town. Before I can even remember when I made my first May Day basket, my brother Nate had started taking baskets to town from our farm for his friends, who were really children of my parents' friends. We had to be about six years old to understand the game.

The object of the May basket exchange was to outrun the recipient before the recipient could catch and kiss the basket taker. We would sneak up to the door of the person getting the basket, knock a time or two and take off as fast as we could before they could catch and kiss us. One of the rules was that you could not start chasing the basket taker until the basket taker had knocked on the door. Of course, if you wanted a kiss from the recipient, you may not run too fast after you knocked on the door!

Nate seemed to always take baskets to Bob, Gene and John for sure, but baskets from boy to boy were more a test of athleticism than a gift to try to get a kiss. Usually they gave one another a punch on the upper arm rather than be seen kissing another boy! If a boy gave a basket to a girl, it was a big clue that he liked her a lot. I know there were a few girls in town hoping for a basket from Nate.

Then, we moved to town when I was about six years old and it was my turn to deliver baskets. Lucy was always a better basket maker than a basket taker. She just could not get into the "chase" of the game. For hours she would cut the baskets, starting with a single sheet of paper; clip the sides evenly after they had been colored with crayons; then fold, form and glue each in place to make the perfect basket with a perfectly proportioned handle, waiting to be filled with a few pieces of candy.

I was the basket filler. I would sort out the piles of like candies, then count one or two of each kind for each basket, making them equal for every recipient. We always made a list ahead of time and each list was comprised of those friends our mothers told us to whom we had to give baskets. Then there was that part of each list we added on of people we especially liked and from whom we wanted to receive a kiss. The lists got longer each year and the chase became more aggressive.

When the baskets were filled and set in a cardboard box in the back seat of the '46 Ford, Mom would decide our route and drive slowly around to each house. The funny part of it was that when we'd pull up in front of the houses with the older girls, they would wait until the very last millisecond when Nate would set the basket down and knock. Then they would take off after him, leaving me behind to watch and see if they could catch him before he got back in the car.

The rule seemed to be that the chasers were not allowed to get inside the cars of the basket droppers. Nate would yell at me to hurry and get in the car before the girls chasing him could catch up and I would see him being kissed. There were a couple of sisters on the north side of town that didn't care who you were; whether you were boy or girl; or even if you completely set the basket down and finished knocking on the door. They would chase us until we were completely out of breath and then pounce on us in the ditch in front of their house.

Even with all the rough and tumble of the game, the ultimate insult was <u>not to be chased</u>! There was a boy from my class who had a heavy crush on me. Mom saw him coming up the path to our house. She thought he was especially cute and smart and happily announced that he was on his way up the path. I swore up and down that I would not chase him or even acknowledge him. She said, "Carol, you have to chase him. He was nice enough to bring you a basket."

I watched as he came slowly up the path with a massive grin on his face, then set down the basket carefully and knocked as loud as he could knock on our front door. He knocked a second time and I didn't answer. He hesitated and I waited. After a few seconds he turned and started back to his mother's car. Mom whispered, "You have to chase him!" So, I opened the door and began a timid lope after him. He slowed up. Then I pretended to see something off to my side and I stopped. He hung his head and got in the car and left. Mom told me that I didn't chase him so I really should not eat the candy in the basket, but I did anyway.

When my Aunt Violet was living with us, she had a similar experience with a young man in town who pursued her. He left her a huge basket with candy, fruit and flowers on the back porch. Mom and I were so impressed with the great gift and wondered why she would not chase him. She said later that she just thought she would go back to Tuttle and marry Vern Ochsner.

Looking back on the May Day tradition, I have often wondered what the dynamic was of the social structure that ruled the day if, in fact, there was one. I wonder why our mothers wanted baskets for some of our friends and not for others. I wondered who started the tradition and by researching the internet, I found that May Day was a Pagan holiday in the beginning, and ended up being mostly a holiday started in Great Britain to welcome in the spring. We did not have a maypole celebration in Fessenden, but other parts of North Dakota celebrated the maypole dance.

Catholics celebrate the month of May as being the Month of Mary and they honor her by crowning her with flowers. I know we looked forward to May Day every year and I am glad our mother made us create our own baskets instead of buying them at the general stores on Main Street.

May Day basket giving usually stopped about age 12 or 13. Why? Probably we were thinking then about getting kisses in a not-so-public way! When we lived in San Diego and May Day came around, I asked if the kids on our street delivered baskets and not a soul knew what I was talking about!

(Published April 18, 2018 in *The Herald-Press*, Harvey, ND.)

Left: Brother Nate and my dog Blackie

Above: Me and Lucy

The Night Before Christmas in Fessenden

*"If Lucille jumped off a cliff,
you'd jump off too!"*
— Famous Emma sayings

Most kids look for any excuse to skip school, but not me. I loved school. Mom said that we were not allowed to go to school when we had the mumps and I guessed she was right. Mumps hurt a little and were boring, especially in a North Dakota prairie town this close to Christmas.

Mom bundled me up like a cabbage roll and sat me in the wooden rocker facing the street by the dining room window. She said I could watch the cars go by. What cars? Everybody was home, who could be, and did not want to take a chance of getting stuck in the four-foot high snow banks. I was paging through *The Night Before Christmas*, an illustrated book with Santa "laying a finger aside of his nose" and "up on the rooftops..." My friend, Lucy, had recited the poem last year at the First Congregational Church and she had said it exactly right.

I began going over it line by line and thought maybe, just maybe, I could memorize it before Christmas. I had not been assigned anything for "saying my piece" at the Christmas Program and when I told Lucy I was thinking about saying *The Night Before Christmas* at the program, she said, "I'll sit right in the front row with you in case you need help." Her mom, Evelyn, was one of the teachers so she could go early and save us the seats.

I loved my outfit with the black vest, red skirt and the matching beanie cap. I always got to wear the long white cotton stockings saved for church instead of the dull brown stockings for school. When I was getting dressed for the program, it hit my brain like ice cubes that the hooks on the elastic garter belt could snap loose and one of the stockings could slide down one leg during the recitation. I decided that if that happened, I would continue on as if it had not happened at all and no one would notice...they would all just be hanging on the next memorized work falling out of my mouth.

We got in the car and while the engine was warming up, Mom noticed she had forgotten her gloves. It seemed she always forgot something on Christmas Eve, the night Santa came to our house while we were at the program. It seemed like forever for her to find the gloves and she ran back to the car laughing, "The gloves were in my pocket the whole time," she said. That was when I was sure she was as nervous as I was and somehow her being nervous calmed me for a few minutes.

Lucy had the seats saved, on the aisle in the first row on the right, as she promised. I kept going over the lines in my head and could not listen to any of the other kids saying their pieces. Then I heard Evelyn say, "Our next recitation is *The Night Before Christmas* by Carol Owen!" I stood right in the center of the aisle, hands at my sides and could hear the words tumbling out of my mouth, "It was the night before Christmas and all through the house..." Every line came out like snow boot tracks evenly spaced in the fallen snow, straight to the end, "and to all a good night!"

I looked down at Lucy and all the blood had run out of her face. Then she slowly grinned as if she had accomplished something special. Perfect! The clapping sounded like it came from inside and outside the little church that seemed to be swept up in a giant snow shovel and dropped right in the middle of the North Dakota prairie. The applause was for me alone and I thought my heart inside my skinny chest would lift me off the floor.

I had to withstand the agony of waiting for the end of the program; getting the obligatory kiss from my old maid Aunt Ruby; and nudging Mom to get done with her niceties to the ladies from the Ladies Aid Society.

My brother, Nate, and I got stuck in the frame of the kitchen door, trying to beat each other to the Christmas tree and dig out our gifts from Santa. Yes, Santa had sneaked in again when we were at the program! How did he always know when we were gone?

(Published December 21, 2013 in *The Herald-Press*, Harvey, ND.)

My Christmas outfit

It's Fair Time!
(Wells County Fair in the '40s and '50s)

"I have hearing aides. Grandpa Kahler called them 'ear phones.'"
— Bits of Wisdom from Carol

We lived in Fessenden, right next to the Wells County Fairgrounds on the outskirts of town and we couldn't wait until fair time. Mom saved up homemade canned goods and planned meals ahead of time. I saved up money and was given 50 cents allowance for each day if I helped with the work, specifically the dish washing. My brother, Nate, got his lot ready for parking on the west side of our property, near the lilac bushes, so he could charge 25 cents per car during the fair days.

Most of my mom's family from Tuttle, North Dakota stayed with us because we lived in walking distance to the fairgrounds. A man who collected the parking fees behind the racetrack attended the back gate to the fairgrounds. When those areas filled up, he locked the gate. We took the opportunity to crawl under the fence and get in for free. Of course, anyone who might have been in the grandstands or near by could see us but we thought we were getting by without being seen.

As many as 20 people stayed at our house during the fair and Mom had to cook, clean and keep everything going every day. Mom reserved one day at the fair for herself and she brought "cold" lunch for everyone. I had to wash the dishes to get that allowance. Grandma Kahler helped with the cooking. Her specialty was German kuchen. She piled a generous topping of filling and fruit on each kuchen. On Mom's day, Grandma watched a show while sitting in the grandstand and saw me emptying the dishwater in the driveway about 2 p.m. She made a lot of points with me for scolding Mom, "For Pete's sake, Emma, how could you let that poor girl do all those dishes. And no help! What's wrong with you?"

Uncle Clifford, too young to drink, but got drunk at the fair anyway, snuck through the basement coal chute and stumbled upstairs where he tripped over the bodies of his relatives asleep on the floor. "Oh, excuse me. Excuse me."

You entered an exciting world when you walked through the gate. Buildings that had been closed all year now welcomed you: The Arts and Crafts Building with prize ribbons for the best entries, The Wells County Museum where some of Grandpa Pierce Owen's things are still on display to this day, Festival Hall, where they had dances, Old Settlers building, farm displays, 4H contests, church dining stands and special booths under the grandstands that could be rented by locals, trying to make a buck or two during that busy time of year.

Mom won the Gold Cup at the arts and crafts show for her crocheted dresser set. We brought our friends inside to show off her gold cup that she had on a shelf at home for many years. Linda Rudel's mom won first prize for a dress she made for Linda, who was about six years old at the time. I was jealous because her mom could follow a pattern even though my mom was a better seamstress (I thought) and didn't follow a pattern.

Next came the Midway where the "Carnies" ran everything. The rides, cotton candy stands, dining stands, toss-a-nickel stands, Hoochie Coochie burlesque dancers, gypsy fortune tellers, freak shows, crazy house, sharp shooter stands (the guns had been made crooked to miss the targets) for teddy bears and other toys. My Uncle Ted said, "I can hit every one of those damn things if I had my own rifle!" My favorite: the Diggers. I lowered a scoop and tried to pick up a toy. One year, I used my whole allowance. I was addicted to the Diggers.

Local owners who had horses in the races and "strangers" who came from out of town tended the racehorse barns. We were not allowed to go near the barns nor allowed to go to the fair late in the evenings when the "Hoochie Coochie" dancers came out to entice men inside where they could see <u>less</u> of their costumes. When I was older, Mom told me the dancers carried venereal diseases, particularly syphilis. Then I heard from my brother Nate, when I was 80 years old, the local men were helping the young boys sneak in under the tent and watch the dancers.

Today, we have come to our senses and know we cannot call anyone a "freak" or say anything about a "crazy house." One of the dwarf fair performers came to the local café where he drank coffee and ate with his feet because he had no arms or hands. We rarely saw black people except the black men who sometimes traveled with the Carnies.

A black group, Preston Love and his Orchestra, played for the dances three years in a row. They were not allowed to stay at the hotel in town. They must have slept in their van. Lucy's dad, Pete Schimke, whose Mobil gas station was just across the street from the fairgrounds, welcomed the musicians to use his service station bathroom. The five fellows took turns cleaning up at the tiny sink. Preston Love went on to be a jazz great, and played for Marvin Gaye, The Temptations, Aretha Franklin, Gladys Knight, Stevie Wonder and several other big names. Did he ever think of Fessenden? Probably not. Summers in the 1950s were lean times for jazz musicians and he was no doubt glad those days were over.

Local Catholic, Lutheran and Congregational church stands competed for a way to fill their coffers once a year. Lucy and I, 14 years old and Congregationalists, had our first chance to waitress at the Congregational Stand. We looked forward to an afternoon of fun because customers paid tips if the service was good and we needed plenty money to spend at the fair after our shift was over. People stood in line waiting for a seat and there seemed to be an order and custom that dictated customers eat at their "own" church stand. They would brag about how much better the food was at "their" stand, even though some of them never ate at the competitor stands to make a comparison. "You should eat at the Catholic stand because they have better cooks!" "No. You should eat at the Lutheran stand because their food is better than yours!"

Lucy and I ran into trouble from the beginning of our waitress jobs. We waited with anticipation as customers filled up the park bench seats and we watched from the kitchen. The head cook, snapped instructions to, "Get hot and take the orders." Lucy asked me if we had anything to write down the orders and I said, "How the heck am I supposed to know? I came here with you. Remember?" The blood in Lucy's face drained and she started slowly toward her table.

We forgot where the orders went and even forgot to pick up the orders waiting in the kitchen. We had lots of complaints about the food being cold, not enough or it wasn't good (the not-good complaint was probably from a Lutheran who sneaked into our stand).

Lucy got Old Fred Aipperspach at her table and he looked at his bowl of chili and shoved it back at her. "What's this? Beans? I didn't order beans. I ordered chicken!" Lucy grabbed the bowl so fast; it spilled on the white paper tablecloth, just missing his wife's flowered dress.

What do you do with a local lady who volunteered to cook but was known for her bad housekeeping? She weighed 300 pounds and wore the same dress for several days in a row. She ended up peeling potatoes in the back of the kitchen. I loved her moxie and gratefulness just to be there with the other women.

The dust from a dirt floor didn't stay there long. I swore 20% of it went home in my shoes and another 20% Lucy took home in her shoes. When our shift was complete, Lucy and I stumbled out the back entrance and headed straight home. No tip money; no night on the midway and early to bed. Lucy and I never had waitress jobs since that day.

Horse races pulled in many people to our fair. My Uncle Bob had a horse called Meadow Bess who had won many races before she ran in Fessenden. My Aunt Stony served as jockey and told Bob, "Those bastards are whipping me instead of their horses. They're jealous because I'm a better jockey!" I thought she was the sexiest woman in our family. She wore her western pants skintight and she had the coolest boots in Fessenden. She took better care of their horses than Uncle Bob who lounged under a shady cottonwood tree drinking a cold Hamm's beer while she walked their horses.

When I was 17, I went to the gypsy fortune teller who waved her hands over her crystal ball and said, "You will have two children. A boy, and two years later, a girl." Well, I did, but there was one boy who slipped between them and he is the one who provided me with my grandchildren. I guess she didn't see him. "Now if you want more information that I see in the crystal ball, it will be another dollar." Curiosity took over and I whipped out another dollar. "You are a hard worker and very trustworthy. In fact, I see you work in an office." That was pretty obvious because I had ink under my fingernails from copying with the mimeograph machine at the Wells County Free Press.

A favorite of the young men was the Demolition Derby. People who wanted to get rid of an old car kept it until fair time and then entered it in the Derby. They smashed the cars into each other until there was only one car left operational and that was the winner. It didn't make much sense to me.

I never understood how the Old Settlers Building got its name. I knew the old people sat on the shaded porch surrounding the building. I also knew I couldn't sit there because I didn't qualify but never knew who actually qualified to sit on those sacred seats. Mom just said, "You can't sit in the Old Settlers Building but you should always smile and wave as you pass by."

When the merry-go-round was being set up the day before the fair, Lucy and I picked our favorite horse. Very often we chose the same horse but then had to choose over until we each picked a different horse. High school kids and adults didn't ride the merry-go-round during the day because that was the time for little kids. Riding in the evening meant you were grown up. My prom date, Jimmy Lloyd, said, "C'mon Carol, let's ride the merry-go-round just for the hell of it!"

When the last day of the fair ended, the Carnies began taking down the midway right away. They had to set up in another town the next day. We woke up the following morning with sad hearts. Next summer seemed a long time away.

(Published June 4, 2022 in *The Herald-Press*, Harvey, ND.)

Summers and the Jim River

"Boys will be boys."
— Unknown Author

Summertime in Fessenden was hot and quiet. Most of the farm kids helped with farm work and harvesting. Those of us who lived in town had little to do after we finished our chores. Saturday was cleaning day at our house and Saturday evenings most people went to town to load up on groceries and visit in the cars, restaurants and bars. Sundays included attending church or a drive in the country. We loved visiting Tuttle, home of my mother's parents. Also, we got to see her other brothers and sisters still living in North Dakota.

Lucy and I still played with dolls to about nine years old and it filled up most of our time. It was interesting, to us anyway. We played "Brownie Scouts" with our dolls and had meetings where we traded off houses about every other day. I called Lucy's mother, Evelyn, at the gas station and told her we were having the "B.S." meeting at my house that day. Evelyn laughed like crazy when she told Lucy what I had said and it took some explanation to get across to Lucy what "B.S." usually meant to older people.

Lucy didn't like swimming and seldom went with us to the James River on the school bus. We called it the "Jim River" located about six miles north of town. Before we left on the school bus, Mr. Killie, the Superintendent of the School, checked the bus to make sure everything and everyone was in good shape. Mom used to shake her head when I packed my lunch that consisted of a mustard sandwich and a cookie. She could not see the nutritional value of the mustard sandwich.

There was a dam on the river; a roped off wading area with a small dock on the river's edge; and a floating dock in the middle of the river. A small building, divided by an inner wall, separated the boys' dressing room from the girls' dressing room. Everyone discovered the punched out knotholes in the divider wall and covered them up before getting undressed. We giggled getting dressed in our bathing suits and raced to the water's edge a few feet away.

Our feet sank up to our ankles in the muddy bottom of the river as we waded in slowly and it seemed like no matter how hot the weather, the water was always cold. The teenagers taught swimming lessons. I could dog paddle but I couldn't float because it freaked me out when my ears filled with water. There was no way I would even think of opening my eyes under the water to take in the murky mess being thrashed around the bottom. I always stayed in the wading area where I could make a quick getaway if the boys started splashing the girls. The worst part of it was when we got a blood sucker on us and it had to be pulled off, or in some cases, touched with a lit match to make it squirm away.

I hoped some day I'd have enough stamina and courage to swim out to the floating dock. There, I dreamed of taking a sunbath with the other girls. I was determined to learn how to swim and even excel at it because most other sports involved grass, dust, or anything that aroused my asthma and hay fever. Sometimes, the older boys would dunk other kids and I guess my turn had come. I was standing in the water talking to Gary Collacker when his brother, Wayne, dived off the floating dock, swam all the way under water, dipped below the rope and pulled my legs out from under me. Gary stood on top of my shoulders and held me down!

I couldn't breathe and everything started turning black in my head as the mud swirled around the bottom of the river. It seemed like I was under water for several minutes, but I'm sure it was just a few seconds. When I came up, I was gasping for air and my lungs were burning. I couldn't stop coughing for a long time. The boys were laughing at my misery. I staggered to shore, curled up, wrapped my arms around myself and held on until I had the strength to get up and creep back to the dressing room where I sat on the bench and waited for the day to be over. Since then, I have always feared a watery death.

(Names in this story have been changed)

The Fight

*"Lucy and I could finish each other's sentences.
We were that close."*
— Bits of Wisdom from Carol

Lucy was my best friend. We were friends from about the age of one and a half. I remember jumping on the couch in their apartment that was in the same building as their gas station and repair shop. It was the cutest apartment I have ever seen and remember every part of it. Her mom, Evelyn, pretty much ran the gas station. She pumped the gas; sold the pop, candy and cigarettes; and kept the books. Pete, Lucy's dad, was the greatest mechanic in Fessenden and spent many hours working on the cement floor of the shop.

Evelyn had been a teacher and would help Lucy study in their car parked outside the station. Lucy was always the smartest student in our class. She was also the shyest person in the school. My mom, Emma, always wondered why my dresses were pulled loose on the left side. After seeing us together, it was obvious that Lucy was hanging on to my dress whenever she wasn't with Evelyn.

I was outgoing and physical feats were important to me. We made a good team: Lucy the shy bookworm and me the physical leader. We were so close; we could finish each other's sentences. It all worked out great until we got into high school and the two characters did not meld.

Each began to go their separate way because we were getting ready to grow up and get ready for adulthood.

Then came the volleyball game in gym class. The teacher had gone through a great deal of preparation setting up the net indoors because we couldn't play outside in the North Dakota snow. Everything had to be set up and taken down in the same day and there would be a basketball game that night.

Lucy and I were on the same side and there were older girls on the other side of the net. We were slamming the ball back and forth and I was in Seventh Heaven because we were tied and had a chance to beat them for the first time since I don't know when. I was up closer to the net and Lucy was way in back where I thought was safest for her to be for a non-athlete.

Unfortunately, the ball whizzed past me and went directly to Lucy, who stood there like a stone and barely bent her wrist to tap on the ball! Dang! The buzzer went off just as she looked around for the closest door to the water fountain, just outside the gym in the hallway.

I was hollering at her all the way to the water fountain, and I could see she didn't give a damn if we lost or won the game. She quietly took her time getting her drink of water and that was the last straw for me. I slammed her head in the fountain and she came up out of there with a whole new personality! She had a crazed look on her face and her long fingernails were clawed and ready to scratch my face, which they did.

The fight was on! Scratching, pushing, and hitting, all while trying to be quiet so Superintendent Killie wouldn't hear us. A crowd of girls began egging us on and told us to get in the locker room and continue the fight. I got in one extra hit on the way in and Lucy had the nerve to slap me back!

I thought the fight was over because Lucy took off for the shower. So, I followed her and we both quietly finished our showers. On the way out of the shower, she shoved me again! Wow! She wasn't done yet, so I shoved her back and we stopped again.

During those years, there were a couple of three-foot by three-foot boxes of foot powder in the locker rooms. She was walking through the foot powder and I gave her a push just so I would get in the last blow. She came back at me and slapped the glasses off my face! I knew what was waiting for me at home when I announced my glasses were going to have to be replaced. Broken glasses. That was enough! So, I returned the slap and broke her glasses. The fight stopped again.

We both finished getting dressed and took off for our history class as the bell rang again. We left the locker room quietly with foot powder scattered all over the floor and never talked about the fight again. There were no apologies or discussions about who won and who lost the fight. The weirdest thing was how the fight started and stopped. Our friendship never suffered from the fight and the friendship has lasted to this day. Written in my 80th year.

(Published November 20, 2021 in *The Herald-Press*, Harvey, ND.)

The fighters

Glenn

"That's what friends are for..."
— Famous Emma Sayings

Glenn Belcher's parents had an insurance agency on Main Street; but then, everything was on Main Street, except the gas stations. Sometimes, his mother would help his dad at the office and we would greet them on Saturday nights when we were walking up and down Main Street. That was a tradition on Saturday nights when everyone came to town to load up on groceries and gas for the week. Sitting around and talking was a huge part of social life in small towns throughout North Dakota.

It was close to Christmas and Glenn's mother, the Superintendent of our Sunday school, had the last word when it came to selecting the pageant characters.

I wanted to be Mary, Mother of Jesus, but I was too shy to ask. My chances were good, though, because the other girls were also shy and the congregation was small. Then, Mrs. Belcher let the information slip out that her son, Glenn, was going to be Joseph. Glenn was a year younger than me so I decided that I was no longer interested in being "Mary." Maybe next year I would be Mary and walk down the main aisle of the church, holding Baby Jesus, beside an older boy.

My friend, Lucy, said that her mother, Evelyn, one of the Sunday School teachers, told Lucy not to tell me, but Glenn was going to be the one to pick his "Mary." The next Sunday after church Mrs. Belcher asked me if I would be Mary in the Christmas pageant. I let my objections go because the next year I might not be asked again.

Mom designed my costume—a plain blue dress and she cut up an old sheet for the white veil. My favorite doll became the Baby Jesus. Glenn and I walked slowly down the aisle and I avoided his hand under my elbow, pretending to be carefully holding the Baby Jesus. Then, I slowly bent over, not showing my back to the congregation as instructed by Mrs. Belcher, and tucked the blankets around the baby in the cradle. On the way out, when everyone was singing "Joy to the World," I could no longer avoid Glenn's outstretched arm and slipped my wrist inside his elbow.

When Glenn had finished his sophomore year and I had finished my junior year in high school, we went to church camp at Lake Metigoshe, near Bottineau, North Dakota. Since we were the only two going to camp, I had to ride with Glenn. His mother was nervous because he had just gotten his driver's license. We hardly talked at all on the way up to camp. Everyone was "pairing off" at camp, but Glenn and I didn't get anyone who wanted to "pair off" with us. The last day of camp, one of the girls came running down to the cabin and said, "Hey, you gotta go up to the rec hall! They're rockin' and rollin' up there!" I rushed to the rec hall and sure enough, the music was LOUD, pounding out "Great Balls of Fire" by Jerry Lee Lewis and everyone was rockin' and rollin.' Glenn grabbed my arm and we rocked and rolled together all afternoon to "Sugartime" by the McGuire Sisters, "Oh Boy" by Buddy Holly, "Wake Up Little Susie" by the Everly Brothers, and my favorite, "Rebel Rouser" by Duane Eddy.

On the way home, we talked non stop about how great camp was and what fun we had rockin' and rollin.' He asked if I'd go with him to a movie some time and I said I would, but when we got back to town, I remembered he was a year younger than me and the movie date never happened.

I moved to California after graduating from high school, and then returned the next summer and got to see a lot of my old friends, classmates and the new graduates. The girls who didn't drink beer were standing around watching the boys drinking beer to show off. Glenn looked at his bottle of beer and said, "I'm going to finish off this bottle of beer if it kills me!" My friend, Lucy, looked at me and said, "And it probably will!" We both laughed and discussed what a cute guy Glenn had turned out to be.

A few years later, I heard from Lucy that Glenn became an Air Force pilot and that everyone in our small town was proud of Glenn's service to our country in the Vietnam War. They even talked about how he took off in his jet from the airport in Grand Forks and formed a ninety-degree angle to show off for his dad. All the old veterans were throwing around words like "Duty," "Honor" and "Country." Many of the protesters of the war threw around other words, like "Politics," "Money" and "Greed."

I was getting married; having babies, trying to get ahead in life and too busy to think much about the harsh reality of the war or the brave men fighting every day for a war that would end in a chaotic defeat. Then, I heard Glenn's plane was shot down, on December 31, 1967. The cockpit was intact, but Glenn's body was missing. That's when the questions started coming to me. Why did this have to happen to our hero? What was this war all about? Who decided it was worth the sacrifice of our young people? Was this the war assigned to our generation?

After the Vietnam Memorial Wall was completed, a replica of it came to San Diego and my friend and I decided to see it at the Navy Hospital near Balboa Park. I searched for over an hour before I found Glenn's name. There it was—the reality of it: Glenn Arthur Belcher, the physical proof Glenn was missing. Why did I cry when I traced his name? Was it his name, or all the names on that black shiny wall?

In 1997 they had recovered his body in Laos and buried it at Arlington National Cemetery on December 31, thirty years to the day of his death. The body of my "Joseph."

(Published April 2, 2022 in *The Herald-Press*, Harvey, ND.)

Glenn Arthur Belcher

The accomplishments noted in the Fessenden High School yearbook, preceded Glenn Belcher's accomplished service with the United States Air Force, serving with the 1st Air Commando Squadron. On Dec. 31, 1967, piloting an A01E Skyraider, call sign "Hobo 19," Belcher left Pleiku, South Vietnam, as the lead of two aircraft on a daylight armed reconnaissance mission against enemy targets in Khammouan Province, Laos. While making its third bombing run at the target, the aircraft crashed for unknown reasons, killing MAJ Belcher. An aerial search was performed but a heavy enemy presence on the ground prevented the recovery of MAJ Belcher's remains at the time. In 1989, the Vietnamese government repatriated human remains believed to be from this loss, and in 1997, U.S. investigators were able to identify MAJ Belcher from these remains.

Excerpts from Defense POW/MIA Accounting Agency

Military record research provided by Anne Ehni,
The Herald-Press, Harvey, ND.

Surprise!

*"It's better to be alone
than in an unhappy marriage"*
— Bits of Wisdom from Carol

After Mom's divorce, we settled into a life of just Mom and us three kids. Mom usually went for coffee at the Connor Hotel Café with her girlfriends. She had made a fur coat for Candy from one of her old fur coats and she would sit Candy in the apple crate she had attached on top of the sled.

Everyone made a big fuss over Candy because she was so cute with her blue eyes and curly blonde hair that would snap back into ringlets. One day, when they got home, Candy started to cry and Mom asked her what was wrong. She said, "None of the ladies said I was cute today!"

Mom was NOT a drinker. She just couldn't drink alcohol but liked to go out with her sisters and girlfriends to Sawyers Bar on Main Street and have a Coke or coffee with them on Saturday night, which was a big night in Fessenden.

Sawyers had hired a new bartender, Elmer Wentz. Mom was there with the Willerts and was feeling brave that night. She decided she would have a couple drinks to show off for Elmer. After midnight, when the bar closed, Elmer offered Mom and the Willerts a ride in his new car and they could go have a cup of coffee at the café. They rode around town for a few minutes and Mom's head started to spin. She knew what was coming and not to damage his new car, she threw up in her coat sleeve!

That was the beginning of their courtship that lasted a few months. When they decided to get married, it was going to happen on the way to Missoula, Montana. Mom made arrangements for our care with Grandma and Grandpa Kahler in Tuttle. We loved it! It was so much fun to stay with Grandma and Grandpa for a few days. They lived across the street from the school and we could have recess all day. We could also go to the stores alone a block away and even sneak into our Uncle Bob's bar and visit a little with the patrons. Uncle Walter Kahler usually stayed with us in Fessenden when he wasn't working and was a big part of our family. Mom and Elmer asked him if he would like to go along and be their witness.

So, they got married on the way to Missoula and Mom's sisters and brothers who lived there gave them a reception. They hung a sheet in the garage of Lydia's house so the pictures of them wouldn't show the back wall of the garage.

The wedding reception cake

Time passed quickly for us with Nate in basketball, football, annual and band. I was a cheerleader, band and choir member and involved in the school newspaper. Both of us were working. Nate worked at the Fairway store and I worked at the Wells County Free Press. Candy was going to school and playing with her girlfriends.

Six years later in the summer of 1957 before my junior year of high school, Nate was preparing for college at Minot State. Aunt Jackie was over for coffee that summer and announced she was pregnant. Later that day, I heard Mom telling Elmer that Jackie was pregnant but she had kept her mouth quiet even though she was pregnant too! Disaster! How could this be? She was too old to have a baby! How embarrassing is this? This is a small town! Everyone will know! What will I tell my friends? Everyone in school will find out! I told my friend Lucy that I wished I was dead!

Mom was tall and slender so her belly didn't pop out like her sister's whose belly ballooned out of shape immediately. So, happily for me, Mom didn't wear maternity clothes that summer. Winter set in and the snow cut like shards of glass through the North Dakota prairie. Then there was Visitors Day for the parents at school. Ms. Pfeiffer had us practice Shakespeare reading the day before with only the best readers in Literature class.

When class started, not one parent was there, so we went ahead and began our readings. We would glance at the door to see if there were any parents coming down the hall. About half way through the class, ONE PARENT walked in the door and it was MY MOM! She had on her maternity top and had braved the storm to visit MY class! Everything changed! From that day on, I told everyone she was pregnant and I couldn't wait for the day our baby was born!

Mom went to the clinic where she told the doctor she was pregnant and thought it might be a good idea to let him know since he would be delivering the baby in Harvey, 17 miles away. He examined her and said, "I don't think you are pregnant. I think you have a tumor." She was so angry, she wouldn't go back and told Elmer, "I have had three children and I guess I know when I'm pregnant. I'm not going back to him until I have the baby."

January 26 was washday. Mom went back to the clinic and said to the doctor, "You know that tumor you said I have? Well, it's ready to come out!" The doctor examined Mom and told her to meet him at the Harvey Hospital immediately. The baby was ready to come out!

Most of the time, Elmer would pick up Candy and me for lunch. He told us what was happening and said that Mom wanted to fix lunch first. She fed us lunch and he took us back to school. She washed the dishes and finished the laundry. They drove to Harvey where the doctor was waiting with his hands scrubbed and ready to deliver her baby. It was a boy and my brother Nate suggested they name him Terrence Elmer. It was the day before her 44th birthday.

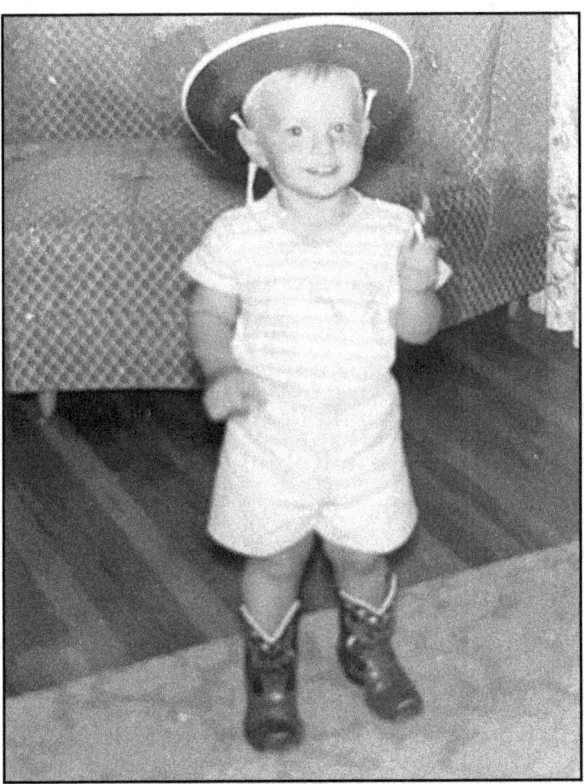

Brother Terry, two years later in San Diego, CA home

Loss of a Child

*"It's the wrong order of things,
when a child dies before his mother"*
— Bits of Wisdom from Carol

When I suspected I was pregnant with our first child, Conrad and I went to see his family doctor. Yes, it was true: we would be having our first child. We were very happy about the good news! The doctor said that he no longer delivered babies; was going to retire soon and recommended Rees-Stealy Clinic on Fourth Avenue near downtown San Diego.

Dr. John Carpenter, OB/GYN was relatively new to his practice and came well recommended. He was incredibly good looking, had a soft-spoken manner and self assurance that made me feel comfortable around him. He said that it would be okay to continue working at Graysons' that was one of a Grayson-Robinson Department Store chain on Fifth Avenue in downtown San Diego. I was the Head Cash Cashier so I did not have to stand for long periods of time during the workday. I immediately got a couple of maternity dresses at the store and couldn't wait to start wearing them. The baby would be born about May 10 the following spring (1963).

We didn't have a car so I took the bus downtown every day to work and Conrad walked the short distance to his work as a Keeper at the San Diego Zoo. He would take a small wire cart to get groceries. I would make the list and give it to him the night I brought home my pay that was in the form of cash ($47/week). As the Head Cash Cashier, I prepared the payroll and stuffed the envelopes for all the employees. The next evening, when I got home from work, the groceries had been hauled home and the things for the refrigerator were put away. The rest of the groceries were set neatly on the kitchen table for my inspection.

Conrad would be sitting in the living room chair in his uniform with work boots laced up, watching television until it was time for bed. It took several years for me to convince him to take off his shoes and relax when he got home from work. We charged the ultra-modern television set on our first credit card at Sears. We didn't go out very often because we had little money left over after paying the rent and buying groceries. We visited family members and watched television for entertainment.

For New Years Eve 1962, we decided to splurge and go with his brother Abe and wife Janice to a dance at the ballroom on Broadway in downtown. I had a new black maternity dress with a straight skirt and slightly flared top that had pink lace on the bodice with a soft chiffon ruffle overlay. The dress had been on layaway at a maternity shop, also on Fifth Avenue, just below Broadway. I got the dress out of layaway a couple days before the dance. We were so excited to get dressed up and go out for a change of pace and night of fun.

It was my day off that New Years Eve day and I went to the Beauty College in Hillcrest to have my red hair put up in a French roll, the latest style. My hairdresser was older than the other students and very, very slow: but she wanted everything to be just perfect and kept waiting between steps to get approval from the teachers before going on with my hairdo. I became very dizzy and had to go to the bathroom to put cold water on my face a couple of times. Little did I know it was an early warning sign of impending doom.

From the Beauty College, I had an appointment to have my picture taken with a coupon I had purchased from one of the ladies at work. It was for an 8x10 picture for $3.00. I remember the photographer telling me to wet my lips before I smiled like I would just before I kissed my husband! (My father-in-law, Sam Grayson, always wanted the picture but it was my only copy so wouldn't let him have it.)

My French roll hairdo

We went to the dance in Abe's new champagne color Chevrolet. He let us ladies out in front and circled the block in search of a parking spot. We had to bring our own bottle, which Abe did, and we could purchase the mixers at the ballroom. The ballroom was upstairs, large, loud and had a layer of cigarette smoke that hung in the air like the low laying fog on the Pacific Coast not far away. Abe and Janice were the sexy dancers and Conrad and I were the smooth dancers. I didn't drink alcohol but had a fifty-cent soda in a small glass. "These glasses are perfect for juice glasses," Janice said.

The night came to an end all too soon and while Janice and I were waiting for our husbands to get the car, we picked up a few glasses to stock our cupboards. It wasn't difficult to hide them in our purses and under our coats but the security guard heard them clink when we were going down the steps to meet the men. He gave us a knowing grin and said, "Good evening, ladies!"

On New Years Day, Conrad had to work and I had housecleaning to do and dinner to prepare. He had given me a new sewing machine for Christmas and said I should not lift it for fear it would be bad for me in my condition. There was a small room off the kitchen and bathroom we had designated as a nursery. There was a little table in the room and under it, he had set the new sewing machine. I thought I had to dust the floor under the table, so I lifted the sewing machine up onto the table.

By the time Conrad got home from work, I was having pressure pain in my groin area. I waited awhile to tell him about it and he said, "I told you not to lift that sewing machine!" Then, the cramps started and I knew disaster was on the way to our unborn child. We called Dr. Carpenter and he told us to meet him at Mercy Hospital.

Conrad called Abe and asked him to take us to the hospital and on the way out the door, I told Abe that I really hurt. I remember worrying that I would get blood or water on his new car. When we arrived, Dr. Carpenter was waiting for us and examined me immediately. He said, "You're losing your baby and I don't know why. You are one of my healthiest patients." I told Dr. Carpenter that I had lifted the sewing machine and he said it would have made no difference—this was going to happen anyway, maybe in two or three days, even if I hadn't lifted the machine.

I asked Conrad to call my mother and tell her what had happened. Dr. Carpenter sat by my bed and he periodically left the room to give an update to Mom and Conrad who were sitting just outside the door. I was having trouble bearing down and finally, Dr. Carpenter told me he was going to leave so I could feel more comfortable alone. He said to press the buzzer and he would be right there waiting for my signal.

After a few tears and feeling sorry for my child and myself, I decided to bear down and do the best I could to have the baby. It wasn't long before I felt something fall between my legs and I heard a squeak like that of a doll or a squeeze toy. I hit the buzzer and Dr. Carpenter rushed into the room. He said the baby was alive but would not live long. I asked him what it was and he said it was a boy as he was leaving the room with the small bundle. I cried and said, "But I heard him! What's going to happen to my baby?" Dr. Carpenter said, "They will dispose of him in the lab." Mom and Conrad came back in and tried to comfort me as best they could and a nurse came in to give me a sedative to help me sleep

In the morning, my mom and stepfather came to see me. A woman from the hospital office came in with a few papers for me to sign. She said that I needed to be moved to a "clean" floor and that this was a floor for babies who had been born full term. Then she asked me who our mortician was and said that I needed to sign the release for them to remove the baby's body from the morgue. I told her that Dr. Carpenter said the baby was going to be disposed of in the lab. She said that the baby had lived for two hours and now had to be buried. I told her I didn't know what my husband wanted to do and I wasn't going to sign the papers. My stepfather said to her, "You don't like your job very well, do you?" With that, she stormed out of the room.

I called the store to tell the Assistant Manager, Mr. Castro, what had happened and that I would not be able to come to work. He said, "You get in here tomorrow or you're fired!" As it turned out later, I did not have to return to work at the store. Ever.

When Dr. Carpenter came in, I told him what had happened with the lady from the hospital office and he said, "Don't worry about it. You're not going anywhere and anyway, I want your husband to see the baby before they take him away. Your baby boy was gasping for air the whole time he was alive because his heart and lungs were not fully developed." I asked if our baby had been baptized and he said that, yes, he had been as there is a Catholic priest at the hospital at all times who baptized him while he was still alive.

Conrad did see our little Shane Christopher, who still had webbed hands and feet; no hair; was one foot long and weighed one pound. I asked Dr. Carpenter if I could see the baby too and he said I could if I insisted but he thought it best I not see Shane Christopher for fear I would have that picture in my mind the next time I got pregnant. I had an incompetent cervix and as soon as the baby had gained weight, I could not sustain him in my body. Otherwise, he was perfectly formed for a baby of about 18 weeks into my pregnancy.

Conrad's father told us not to worry about a thing—that he would handle all the details and pay for everything. An argument ensued at my bedside and Conrad said, "I can bury my own child." That is exactly what he did. We buried our child at Holy Cross Cemetery in San Diego. Although I never saw the casket, it was three feet long, white and had a small satin pillow for his little head.

When I called the store again after I got home, I spoke to the Manager, Mr. Goldfarb, who said, "You go ahead and collect your unemployment, honey. Take care of yourself." Ramona Paulson, my Maid of Honor at the wedding and my friend from work, came to visit me and said that I was lucky I wasn't working at the store any longer. She said that Mr. Castro had been caught embezzling through the credit accounts and when he was arrested, he said that the girls in the credit department were framing him because he was having an affair with every one of them! It wasn't long after that the store closed.

My body knew the baby was born, so began producing milk. I would lay towels under me at night and woke to find them soaked with milk in the morning. I cried and grieved for the loss of my first child. Dr. Carpenter said that I could still get pregnant and there was a new shot that would help strengthen my cervix, hopefully long enough for my next child to survive on its own.

Then the nightmares began. I dreamed that Shane Christopher was standing next to the bed in yellow pajamas tugging at the blankets, wanting his milk. I would wake up sweating, leaking milk and crying. In my nightmares, he was the same size as when he had been born: only a foot tall and only one pound. Sometimes I wished Dr. Carpenter hadn't discouraged my seeing Shane Christopher because my nightmares were probably more frightening to me than what he no doubt looked like in the morgue.

When we had our taxes prepared for that year, the tax preparer said we could claim Shane Christopher as a dependant because he had drawn a breath of life. I do not want this child to be forgotten.

My Uncle Arnie

*"When the chips were down,
he came through!"*
— Famous Emma Sayings

Arnie was a devoted husband to Aunt Helen and good father to her sons, Gerald and Dennis. The boys' father, Bernard Albright, died in Missoula, Montana while fighting a grocery store fire in 1952. Arnie Beich and Helen were married on August 13, 1956 at St. Anthony's Catholic Church, in Missoula.

I was 18 years old and staying with Helen and Arnie for a few months after we moved to San Diego. Arnie called and said, "Fix rice and leftover roast. Helen has to work late." I put the water on to boil and when I added the rice, it didn't do much, so I added more and more. By the time she got home, the rice was pouring over the edge of the 16-quart canning kettle. I felt terrible and almost cried. He said, "That's okay, Carol, I love rice." He gobbled down most of it that night and finished it off the next night!

Uncle Arnie and Aunt Helen were a match. Arnie always paid his own way and went out of his way to see that everyone was comfortable in his home. Arnie was generous and kind. He loved children and children loved him. They felt safe around him because he was non-threatening and approachable. Arnie was my godfather when I was baptized in the Catholic faith at age 19.

Though quiet, Arnie was easy going and made friends quickly. Arnie loved to fish, camp, meet friends at the VFW and search for bargains at the grocery store so he could "stock up."

Family members said that at just age 16, Arnie served in the Marines in WWII at Guadalcanal with the 3rd Amphibious Marines when the United States was at war with Japan in the Pacific Ocean on the Solomon Islands Campaign. Arnie ate anything and everything, EXCEPT figs and bananas because there were some days when that's all he had to eat during that Campaign.

Helen died of cancer in early 2004. Arnie guarded, protected and cared for her to the end. He was never the same after she died. While showing me his food storage, he said, "I stocked up on groceries a long time ago so Helen wouldn't have to go to the store so much after I died." He got a lump in his throat and blurted out, "I was supposed to die first, you know."

The night Arnie died, I took a notebook and pen to with me to Mimi's Restaurant to start documenting his story for the World War II Memorial. He said Dennis had his discharge papers with all that information. I told him I wasn't particularly interested in the statistical stuff. I wanted to hear his story.

We hear a lot these days about war and heroes but like a true hero usually does, he just said:
- that he didn't do anything different than the other guys;
- he just did his job;
- the other Marines knew what he did and that was enough for him.

The minute dinner was served, Arnie had his first spell (mild seizure?) and I was not able to get the rest of his story. I should have known, when he couldn't eat his dinner, that something was very wrong. I begged him to let me call an ambulance or stop at the sheriff's substation but he said he just wanted to get home.

My Uncle Arnie died the same way he lived:
- trying not to bother anyone;

- not asking for anything;
- no complaining;
- suffering in silence;
- paying his own way and
- getting it over with quickly.

I am sure Arnie would have liked more privacy his last hour but I was too much in a state of shock at the sudden onslaught of things. I thought I could save him. No doubt, he is buying a round of drinks for everyone beyond the Pearly Gates. He and Helen are in good company.

Aunt Helen and Uncle Arnie

I'm in Jail!

"Some family members are crooks!"
— Bits of Wisdom from Carol

"Don't do the crime if you can't do the time!" The quote from Baretta, American Detective series that appeared above the outer sally port gate at the San Diego County Jail greeted workers checking in for a day of work. It could also be seen by visitors just off to the side who checked in to visit their friends and loved ones incarcerated at the old Central Detention Facility downtown.

This was the eighties and the jail suffered from age. The pistol range downstairs offered the deputies a chance to practice their marksmanship. They said the cockroaches were so big they could shoot them with their guns.

I checked in the first day for work as a Jail Clerk after passing the test with 499 others. I was number four on the list and hired first after three candidates above me failed the drug test. I was very aware of the tight security and risk taken by the deputies as they placed their weapons in the sally port slots. The second gate creaked open and we proceeded inside, each to our work areas.

Seasoned Jail Clerks did most of the training of newcomers. A deputy questioned my abilities. The senior clerk told him, "Don't worry about her. She's going to be good." I <u>was</u> a good Jail Clerk and knew my place in the social order of the jail, however, I took a stand for a newer, younger clerk when I was the senior clerk on duty and I didn't like the way she was treated by a couple officers. My stand was quickly noticed and my complaint was quickly resolved. It was gratifying to help her later in her personal life

Jail clerks were required to check and review inmate charges and bail amounts that were public information available to bail bondsmen, attorneys and the general public. With proper identification, the jail clerks set up visitation. The windows were always open to receive bail amounts and for the clerks to put money "on the books" for the inmates. Mail and some personal items for the inmates were allowed after being checked by the clerks. The deputies checked suspicious items, such as shoes with possible intravenous needles buried in the innersoles.

Many times, street people and former inmates would break the law to get a place to eat and sleep. Late one evening, a former inmate approached a visitor window and when the clerk asked him what he wanted, he laid a part of his anatomy on the window ledge she didn't want to see. She screamed and ran in the watch commander's office. The former inmate had accomplished his purpose and slept on a warm bed for the night. He ate a perfectly balanced breakfast the next morning ordered by the County Jail Nutritionist.

A couple years later, I easily passed the test for Booking Clerk and began interviewing men who had been arrested in the County, by the San Diego Police or brought in from court. I quickly learned not to maintain eye contact unless I was actually booking an inmate. I took pride in that I booked every man brought to my window. The secret was to continue asking questions and not get involved in trivial conversation or unnecessary criticism from the inmates. If an inmate started to get off track, I would hesitate briefly, and ask him if he would like to deal with me or deal with the deputies. They <u>always</u> chose dealing with me.

Years later, when taking a course in writing, I wrote a piece called "Jail Social Structure" in which I said, "The Watch Commander is

GOD for that day and that shift. Don't think for one minute that his superior officers run the jail because they are seldom even seen in the jail. No matter what happens inside the jail, the Watch Commander makes the rules and sees to it they are enforced. If mistakes are made, the Watch Commander is held accountable. If everything runs smoothly, it is the Watch Commander who has set the tone for good deportment. I think the strength of the Watch Commander is the most important element in jail life."

Deputies are the next in order on the social structure who must be aware, smart and in top physical condition to maintain order because sometimes a deputy will do battle with an inmate. After a fight, the jail becomes a tomb and only the clanging of gates and rustling of inmate release can be heard.

Most deputies knew I had been married to one of their own and that he trained most of them in the academy. They also knew I was dating a District Attorney Investigator, working across the street from the jail. There had been something on the news about Elvis Presley and it was a slow night at the jail. One of the very new deputies saw that I wasn't busy and asked me, "Have you ever seen Elvis Presley?" I said with a straight face, "Well yes. He's the father of my oldest son!" He ran back over to a group of deputies and I could see them laughing at him. He came back to my window and said, "You're a liar!"

I said in my essay that the inmate population is at the bottom of the social structure in the jail. Some people think that a short stint in the County Jail is just what *someone else* needs to teach him or her a lesson. What they don't know is that a short stint in jail can be damaging and even life threatening, especially the first day or two of incarceration.

Jail is the last place anyone should want to be; however, if you should happen to find yourself in this unlikely place, it's important that you understand what you're getting into and how to come out of the experience as unscathed as possible.

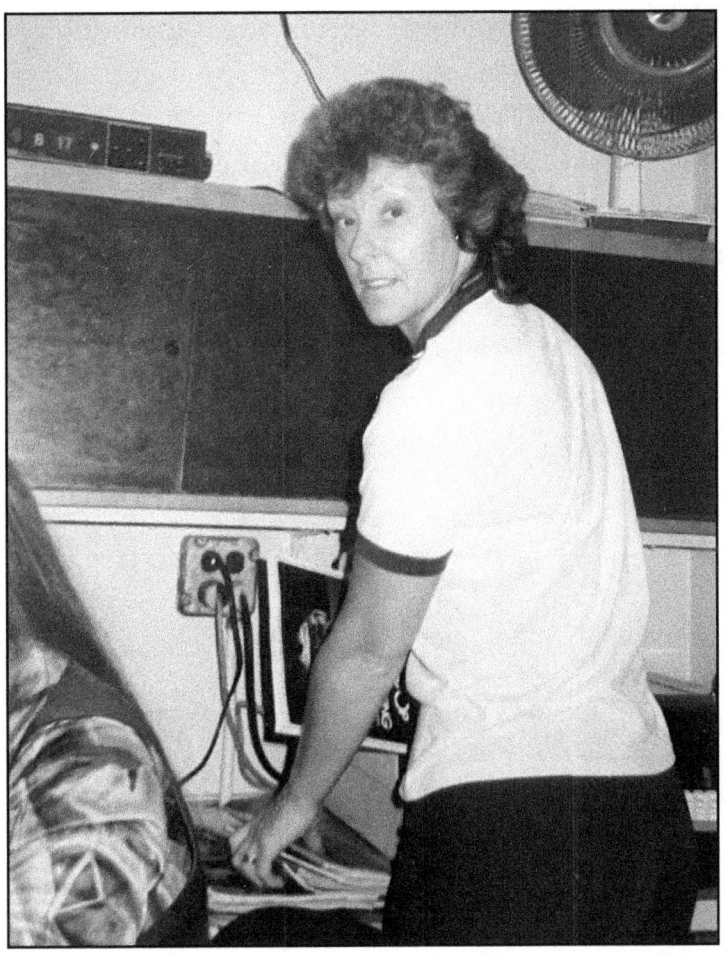

If you should find yourself on the wrong side of the law, do not argue with a deputy or a member of the working jail staff. It would behoove you to just go along with the program and try to get out as quickly as possible. The more you go against the system, the longer it takes to get out. Paperwork cannot be finished when deputies and staff are arguing or fighting with you.

If your loved one calls you from jail, do whatever is necessary to get him or her out. You can inflict your own punishment or make an argument when the time is safe. I don't think jails should be nice places that you want to visit, but we must keep in mind that sometimes innocent people are incarcerated and their rights must be protected. So don't argue with a law enforcement officer and stay out of the lower level of the jail social structure!

My time at the Central Detention Facility in San Diego was interesting and educational. I always said I should have kept notes but I'm afraid much the dark side of jail life would haunt me, so here's what I came up with to avoid documenting any dark time at that facility.

Ms. Macbeth

"Never marry a man with bad credit!"
— Bits of Wisdom from Carol

We were lucky in the fifties to have Elizabeth Pfeiffer, our English/Literature teacher, who cared enough to prepare us for life beyond the books. She taught us to glean whatever we wanted from the books. She was pretty much the "Internet of Yesterday."

One of the things our teacher taught us was to interpret Shakespeare. I heard a lot of groans when she said, "Today, we will not only read, but interpret each phrase of *Macbeth*." Bill Bakken was never chosen to read because she relied on him to interpret when no other classmate "got it." He sat quietly (always) and slowly told us what old Mr. Shakespeare said. 45 years later, I was the "Bill Bakken" of our college class in California.

2005: Hot! And dry! That's the Arizona desert. But I'm tooling along at 70 miles per hour in my 1994 Ford Taurus on the way from San Diego to Phoenix. Divorced again, I have to travel solo. Can't wait to get into the cool air conditioning of my brother Nate's home. Sister-in-law Jeannette's house is always clean, comfortable and she serves great food.

Nate gives me a short tour of their new place and shows me my room. Everything is decorated to serve their western motif, down to the western hand lotion. I love it here. I have no worries because my life is in order and I have all my rehearsing and studying done for my Public Speaking Semester Exam at Grossmont College in El Cajon, California.

I will be giving a "Persuasion Speech" by Lady Macbeth. I have a couple of props: a picture of Shakespeare and a picture of the Thrust Stage used in Shakespeare's day. My persuasion is "Why everyone should study Shakespeare and learn how to be an actor." The famous Sleepwalking Scene in Act V will top off the presentation. Lady Macbeth's hands are dripping with blood. My audience will have to imagine the actual blood. She is cussing at her Lord.

Acting class, two years prior to my public speaking class, has me well prepared to show the young kids in my class how to put themselves in the shoes of another person. I have memorized my piece completely. I have blocked all my moves. I will blow them out of their seats with this presentation.

After my three-day visit, I have the car gassed up and ready for the six-hour trip back to the college. I should have time for a nap before my four o'clock class.

Everything is smooth and steady. I even stop in Dateland, Arizona for one of their famous date malts. Back on the road and still plenty of time to get to the college. I can see the United States Border Patrol Annex, Yuma. The car isn't sounding good. Probably just overheating from the 110-degree heat. Everything gets quiet and I slowly inch into the station side yard. The car stops.

This cannot happen. I just paid off my credit card and I have a deadline in El Cajon. The Border Patrol Agent comes running over and says, "Lady, you can't stop here. You have to go through the checkpoint and be inspected!" I tell him I can't move the car another foot. The engine has quit on me. He asks me what I am going to do and I am thinking, "What the hell does he think I'm going to do, wave a magic wand and go on?"

Another agent comes out and suggests I go inside where it is air-conditioned. I guess he could see my red face and the sweat rolling off me, soaking up my new t-shirt. The second agent suggests we call a tow truck out of Yuma and I agree. An hour later, the tow truck arrives and the driver hooks up my old Taurus. He says, "Hop in lady. Where do you want to go?" I told him I actually wanted to go to El Cajon so I wouldn't miss my class. After comparing the cost, I opted to have him take me back to Yuma for repair. He said, "Do you want an expensive, reliable repair or a cheap reliable repair?" I chose the cheap repair.

We pulled into a gas station on the outskirts of Yuma. The cars were lined up and about 29 men were working on cars and pumping gas. The young lady in the office had to check my credit card to see my limits. I was in great shape credit-wise. I asked the manager how long he thought it would take and he said, "You are third in line for repair. A lot depends on what's wrong with your car." I told him I didn't ask for preferential treatment often but I had to be in El Cajon by 4 p.m. He said I could wait in the employee area just outside the office and feel free to have a little lunch that the employees shared. The beans, rice and tortillas looked good but I didn't like so many flies hanging around the open containers.

The manager returned after about an hour and said the transformer had blown. There was a new one in Downtown Yuma and he would be back in about an hour to complete the repair. No choices now. I was stuck. Good thing I brought my books.

After about another two hours, I signed the credit slip, jumped back in the car and tromped on the gas. The Border Patrol Agents gave me a friendly wave as I left the Annex and I, again, hit the gas hard when I was out of their sight.

The parking lot at the college was full but I didn't care. It was 3:55 p.m. and I might just make it in spite of my sweat-stained shirt and wet hair. The bell went off just as I opened the classroom door! Guess who was first up for the presentations? I made my Introduction; gave my Argument; showed my Props; and Concluded.

Yet here's a spot.

Out, damned spot! out, I say!—One: two: why, then, 'tis time to do't—Hell is murky!—Fie, my lord, fie! A soldier, and afeard? What need we fear who knows it, when none can call our power to account?—Yet who would have thought the old man to have had so much blood in him.

The thane of Fife had a wife: where is she now?— What, will these hands ne'er be clean?—No more o' that, my lord, no more o' that: you mar all with this starting.

Here's the smell of the blood still: all the perfumes of Arabia will not sweeten this little hand. Oh, oh, oh!

Wash your hands, put on your nightgown; look not so pale.—I tell you yet again, Banquo's buried; he cannot come out on's grave.

To bed, to bed! There's knocking at the gate: come, come, come, come, give me your hand. What's done cannot be undone.—To bed, to bed, to bed!

Perfect! Standing ovation! I got an "A."

Surgery Awry!

"Never trust a doctor who is going on vacation the next day."
— Bits of Wisdom from Carol

June 9, 2011

Dear Deaton,

    I had to write and let you know I almost died! I went in for a 4-hour hemorrhoidectomy (that started about noon on May 2) and ended up spending three days in the hospital. The priest even came up and anointed me! My friend, Eileen (the one from up there near Boston) said that I am the only person she has known who went in for a hemorrhoidectomy and ended up with the last rites!

    Anyway, I started hemorrhaging and they had to admit me to the hospital. I told Chuck and John to leave late in the evening because I was tired. Then, all hell broke loose. I called for the nurse and told her I had to get up because I could feel the blood coming out. She said, "I'm sorry, but you can't get out of bed." Then she started to walk away and I said, "If I lay here and bleed to death, is that what you're going to say, *I'm sorry?*" She said, "Yes, that's what I'm going to say. I'm sorry." I said, "Who are you going to say it to?" She got ticked off and spun around and said, "I'll get you a rep." (She never did)

So, I hit the button again and told them I was getting up and two nurses and two techs came in and when I stood up the blood just shot out of me, across the room, and one of the nurses even had to change her uniform!

One of techs grabbed a thick bed pad and was going to wipe it up and the older nurse said, "Just leave it there so she can see it." I presumed she meant the nurse who was in earlier.

They monitored me every 15 minutes for about 3 hours and then I had a seizure. My legs flopped all over the place; I was sweating and vomiting and they said my eyes were popping out of my head! As much faith as I think I have, I didn't even think about God. I guess the human survival instinct just took over and all I could think of was, "If I can just stop my legs from flopping around, I will live." Eventually, of course, I held my legs as tight as I could and the seizure stopped. They cleaned me up again, as best they could, and monitored me again for about an hour when I called them and said, "I'm going to the bathroom." All four rushed in again and I stood up and hemorrhaged again and began slipping in it. They made me lay down and cleaned me up again.

About 4:30 a.m. the doctor came in and said, "I forgot to tie off a couple things and we are going to have to do a second surgery." He said that when they do that kind of surgery, they lay you flat on the table and even put you upside down, and that when I stood up, all the blood just came out! He didn't even say he was sorry. They called John, who picked up Chuck, and they took me off before the guys could get there. They did the second surgery on Tuesday morning at 5 a.m.

Then the doctor went on vacation and left me to his associate who I never saw. The educator from the church was making her communion rounds and saw my name on the list. She took one look at me and called the priest, who came up and anointed me!!!!! I said that if he could stand the smell in that room, he's a better person than I am!

I went home on Wednesday and was still bleeding on Friday, so called the associate who was too busy to see or talk to me, so I called him at 3 a.m. and he HAD TO TALK TO ME. He said that if I was worried about too much bleeding, to go to the emergency room, which I did, and when it was time to go back to the original doctor, I refused to see either one of them and ended up seeing still another associate of theirs, who was very nice, but tried three times to get me to see the original doctor, which I have not done and will not do.

The nurse in the office said that I should see the original doctor because he was "One of the best surgeons in this area and people are standing in line to see him." I told Chuck that if I'd thought of it, I should have said that someone else can have my place in line. I tried to not even go back to that office, but she said that I HAD to see a surgeon, not my regular doctor, for GET THIS:

"Insurance purposes and for HIS protection!"

So that's the end of my story.

- *Carol*

A Big Heart

"He's the best thing since sliced bread"
— Famous Emma Sayings

Ken's old heart was the largest enlarged heart ever removed at Vanderbilt, Nashville at the time by that surgeon. A 52-year-old man donated the heart, and gave Ken a new life. Only one doctor gave him a 10 percent chance of living TO the transplant. The <u>Doctors of Little Faith</u> didn't give him that much of a chance. After the surgery, one of the nurses asked him if he had been afraid before the surgery and he said, "I thought, while being wheeled down to surgery, there were only two ways this could go: I could be given a fresh new life or live in the next dimension that I call Heaven. I was at peace like no other time in my life."

Heart problems can be genetic, yes, but strength of character, lots of prayer and a determined, loving wife were no doubt the keys to saving Ken's life. Susan prepared her man and herself to be ready when the call from Vanderbilt on June 12, 2016 came in to be at Nashville Vanderbilt in four hours to get his new heart. They had to be at Tri Cities Airport in one hour to catch an AirMed flight with a registered nurse on board to care for Ken. Inclement weather and arrangements for the donor to pass hesitated the process but two days later, on June 14, 2016 Ken got his new heart, just in time to meet the transplant deadline of age 70 then in effect.

The <u>Doctors of Little Faith</u> tried to side step the transplant because of Ken's fragile condition. They had not bargained on Ken's wife, Susan who even followed a doctor down a hallway, insisting, "He can make it! You can save him!" These same doctors thought it a useless surgery because they had predicted he would be dead in another one to two weeks with a heart that had been functioning at only 11 percent before the operation.

The Navy doctor did not indicate Ken's heart condition at his retirement examination from the Navy in 1985 because last minute orders had sent Ken to inspect aircraft in Naples, Italy, Rota, Spain and Sigonella, Sicily. In order to meet the deadline for his retirement from the military, he was discharged without a complete examination that would have qualified him for disability. Fortunately, Ken is now covered by Tri-Care for Life, an excellent health insurance, and eligible at age 65.

After retirement from the Navy, Ken went to work at Northrop Grumman as an Aircraft Electronics Representative coordinating with Navy personnel. High blood pressure was an impediment during an application for a home loan a few years later in Chesapeake, Virginia. To others, his blood pressure counts were high, but to Ken these high counts were normal for him. Ken in his mid forties had been given blood pressure medications and the doctor approved the loan.

While working in Ocala, Florida about 2000 to 2005, Ken suffered congestive heart failure twice in one week, and had a pacemaker installed because his heart was functioning at only 14 percent. This pacemaker contained three wires and would conceivably control atrial fibrillation until a new heart was available. A Left Ventricular Assist Device (LVAD) heart pump was offered in the fall of 2015. Ken thought he would be too weak for two surgeries. Milrinone, a medication for cardiac support in patients with acute heart failure, pulmonary hypertension, or chronic heart failure, was used until the heart transplant that kept Ken alive until he got that magic call on June 12, 2016.

Prayer lists for Ken's recovery were held at several churches, St. Anne Catholic Church in Bristol and at the East End Baptist Church in Marion, Virginia that was built in part by Ken's grandfather. Praise God![1]

(Above Left) Ken Johnson in his Navy Uniform.
(Above Right) Ken after his heart transplant surgery, circa 2018.

---

1 I married Ken Johnson (2019) after the deaths of Chuck (2015) and Susan (2017).

Pictured – Left to Right: Mary Jo, Ken's nephew's wife; Lyndia, Ken's sister-in-law; Ken, before transplant surgery; and Ken's mother, Dorothy.

East End Baptist Church, Marion, VA

Terms & Definitions

1 - *A Stormy Birth*
Emma Owen - My mother. Maiden name Kahler
Newt Owen - My father. Newton
Nate - My brother. Nathan
Uncle Bill - My dad's brother. William
Aunt Ida - Bill's wife
Marlys and **Beverly** - Bill and Ida's daughters

2 - *May Day*
Bob, Gene and **John** - Nate's friends
Lucy - Lucille Schimke - My best friend
Aunt Violet - Violet Kahler. My mom's sister

3 - *The Night Before Christmas in Fessenden*
Old Maid Aunt Ruby - My dad's sister

4 - *It's Fair Time!*
Grandma Kahler - My mother's mother
Uncle Clifford - Kahler. My mother's brother
Linda Rudel - Lucy and my friend. Married Bill Bakken
Uncle Ted - Kahler. My mother's brother
Uncle Bob - Kahler. My mother's brother
Aunt Stony - Kahler. Uncle Bob's wife

5 - *Summers and the Jim River*
Gary and Wayne Collacker - Brothers. Names have been changed for obvious reasons

6 – *The Fight*
Pete – Schimke. Lucy's dad. Evelyn's husband

7 – *Glenn*
All characters are self explanatory

8 – *Surprise*
Candy – Candace Owen Swift. My sister
Elmer Wentz – My stepfather. My mother's second husband
Willerts – Friends of Mom and Elmer. Their son, Ben graduated with me
Uncle Walter – Kahler. Mom's brother
Aunt Jackie – Mom's sister
Terry Wentz – Terrence Elmer Wentz. My brother

9 – *Loss of a Child*
Conrad – Grayson. My first husband. Father of my children
Shane Christopher – Grayson. Our first child.

10 – *My Uncle Arnie*
Arnie – Beich. Husband to my mother's sister
Aunt Helen – Kahler. Mom's sister
Gerald and **Dennis** – Albright. Helen's sons of her first husband Bernard

11 – *I'm in Jail!*
All characters are self explanatory

12 - Ms. Macbeth
English/Literature teacher – Elizabeth Pfeiffer.
Bill Bakken – Classmate. He and Lucy tied for Class Victorian in 1959
Divorced again – Referencing second marriage
Jeannette – Nate's wife. My sister-in-law

13 - *Surgery Awry!*
Deaton – My dear California friend, now deceased. Dang! I miss her
Eileen – My dear California/Massachusetts friend. Dang! I miss her
Chuck – My third husband, now deceased. Bless his heart
John – My son. Father of my grandchildren Meta and Alexander

14 - *A Big Heart*
Ken Johnson – My husband. Married in 2019 after the deaths of Chuck Reynolds (2015) and Susan (2017)
Doctors of Little Faith – Vanderbilt heart surgeons
Tri-Cities Airport – Between Bristol, TN/VA (my town) and Johnson City, TN
Not Surprised Wife – Susan Johnson, now deceased. Ken's first wife
Pictured – Ken in his Navy Uniform
Pictured – **Left to Right:** Mary Jo, Ken's Nephew's wife; Lyndia, Ken's Sister-in-law; Ken, before transplant surgery; Ken's Mother, Dorothy
Pictured – Ken after transplant surgery, circa 2018

Acknowledgments

I would like to acknowledge and thank:

Lucy Bell for her friendship, love, patience and neverending "worry" about me.

Ken Johnson for all the encouragement, support and love during this process of writing my first book. Giving me time and assurance that I can do this when I had my doubts.

Anne Ehni for her appreciation and publishing my "little stories" in *The Herald-Press*, Harvey, ND.

Shane Michael Grayson, John Scott Grayson, Connie Grayson Criswell, Meta Grayson and Alexander Grayson Brown: my children and grandchildren for telling me I have great stories and to write a book.

Nate Owen, my brother, for allowing me to show you part of his life too.

www.ingramcontent.com/pod-product-compliance
Lightning Source LLC
Chambersburg PA
CBHW060034180426
43196CB00045B/2682